CONTE[NTS]

Anlaby Primary School, Hull

Layton Mark Abblett (6)	1
Tyler Burrluck (7)	2
Isabella Rimmer (6)	3
Nicolé Howley (6)	4
Jessica Imogen Overfield (6)	5
Ruby Brooks (7)	6
Matthew White (6)	7
Lily Blair (6)	8
Ryan Fletcher (6)	9
Savannah Goodfellow (6)	10
Maya Casey (6)	11
Amelia Stubbs (6)	12
Theo Lee (6)	13
Libby Winter (6)	14
Oliver Fitzsimmons (6)	15
Doll Peaches (6)	16
Faith Ellerington (7)	17
Romi Western (6)	18
Quinn Graham (6)	19
Alexander Logan Sanders (6)	20
Jared Morgan (6)	21
Aarrison Morris (7)	22
Chloe Edge (7)	23
Ollie Soper (6)	24
Callum James Mainprize (6)	25
Lottie Appleyard (6)	26
Saffron Annabelle Jones (6)	27
Holly Danby (6)	28
Reuben Houlder (6)	29
Edward Hill (6)	30
Evie Minns (6)	31
Scarlett Fitzsimmons (6)	32
Abbie Sullivan-Coles (6)	33
Oscar Swailes (6)	34

Bedale CE Primary School, Bedale

Mia Elizabeth Armstrong (6)	35
Amy Louise Draper (6)	36
Amy Hannington (6)	37
Emmy Stinson (6)	38
Beatrice Hayes (6)	39
William Hearne (6)	40
Alfie Coxon (6)	41
Freddie Cuthbert (5)	42
Joshua Gaskell (7)	43
Leah Knight (6)	44
Walter Oldham (6)	45
Henry James King (7)	46
Kairi Buckton (5)	47
Sophia Ava Read (5)	48
Evie Tate (6)	49
Sarah Nolan (6)	50
Ava Furlong (5)	51
Emily Kingdon (5)	52
Ellie Croft (5)	53
Freddie Crowe (6)	54
Jakob Neate (5)	55
Ava Mollie Prisk (6)	56
Theo Kenny (6)	57
Sydney Schofield (6)	58
Zach Main (5)	59
Wilf Monkhouse (5)	60
Joel Matthew Holloway (6)	61
Esmae Grace Potter (6)	62
Ellis Laing (6)	63
Charley Caygill (5)	64
Harry William Corner (6)	65
Tegan Rachel Selby (6)	66
Jesse-James Freddie Watson (5)	67

Isobel Hainge (5)	68
James Dickinson (6)	69
Fraya Pritchard (6)	70
Poppy Grace King (5)	71
Ava Waldron (6)	72
Harri James (5)	73
Jessica Louise Scarce (5)	74
Courtney Cooper (6)	75
Arthur Nicholson (6)	76
Harry Balsillie (5)	77
Payson Carney (5)	78
Katie-Beth Miller (5)	79
Freya Doyle (6)	80
Mason Tuplin (5)	81
Abby Stewart (6)	82
Jack Allen (6)	83
Tiana Mae Merkin (5)	84
Sam Simpson (5)	85
Grace Lily Kent (5)	86
Levi Chilcott (6)	87
Heather Elsie Hobson (6)	88
Abigail Dakota Butterworth (6)	89
Sophia Teer (5)	90
Sienna Kirkley (5)	91
Kira Graham (5)	92
Evie Graham (6)	93
Thomas Cope (6)	94
Olivia Harker (6)	95
Emily Rebecca Taylor (5)	96
Oscar Byers (5)	97
Jack Thornton-Grace (5)	98
Mia-Louise Fitch (5)	99

Golden Flatts Primary School, Hartlepool

Ally Johnson (7)	100
Taio Hill-Bate (6)	101
Darcie Davies (7)	102
Lydia Evans (6)	103
Abbie Morris (7)	104
Amelia-Mai Pearson (7)	105
Lucianna Ness (7)	106
Grace Olivia Bell (7)	107

Louis Michael Souter (7)	108

King Street Primary School, Spennymoor

Jamie Atkinson (5)	109
Jenson Horniman (6)	110
Elliott Bright (5)	111
Nell Beasley (6)	112
Tabitha Violet Daley (5)	113
Harry Luther (5)	114
Jake David Murdoch (5)	115
Willow Flatman (5)	116
Blake Robert Barnes (6)	117
Katharine Gardner (5)	118
Alfie-Shay Simpson (5)	119
Kellan Bates (5)	120
Amelie Elliott (5)	121
Amelia Dixon (5)	122
Cayden Dodds (5)	123
Scarlett Ellis (5)	124
Danny Summerson (5)	125
Sophia Cathrine Janette Byrne (5)	126
Phoebe Cullum (5)	127
Hayden Parker (5)	128

Our Lady Of The Most Holy Rosary RC Primary School, Billingham

Ethan Jack Harrison (6)	129
Jessica Caitlyn Bruce (6)	130
Zak Georgiou (6)	131
Caitlin Louise Black (7)	132
Georgia Catherine Jackson (6)	133
William Sotheby (6)	134
Tyler Leighton-Spence (6)	135
Mateusz Michal Odziomek (7)	136
Oliver Evans (6)	137
Zara (6)	138
Freddie Harrison (6)	139
Jade Cater (6)	140
Harry Faso (6)	141

Little RIDDLERS

The North East

Edited By Donna Samworth

First published in Great Britain in 2018 by:

YoungWriters

Young Writers
Remus House
Coltsfoot Drive
Peterborough
PE2 9BF
Telephone: 01733 890066
Website: www.youngwriters.co.uk

All Rights Reserved
Book Design by Ashley Janson
© Copyright Contributors 2017
SB ISBN 978-1-78896-076-2
Printed and bound in the UK by BookPrintingUK
Website: www.bookprintinguk.com
YB0344R

FOREWORD

Dear Reader,

Welcome to *Little Riddlers - The North East*, are you ready to get your thinking caps on to puzzle your way through this wonderful collection?

Young Writers' Little Riddlers competition set out to encourage young writers to create their own riddles. Their answers could be whatever or whoever their imaginations desired; from people to places, animals to objects, food to seasons. Riddles are a great way to further the children's use of poetic expression, including onomatopoeia and similes; as well as encourage them to 'think outside the box' by providing clues without giving the answer away immediately.

All of us at Young Writers believe in the importance of inspiring young children to produce creative writing, including poetry, and we feel that seeing their own riddles in print will keep that creative spirit burning brightly and proudly.

We hope you enjoy riddling your way through this book as much as we enjoyed reading all the entries.

Samuel Turnbull (6)	142
Bayleigh Jasmine Violet Henderson (6)	143
Matthew Jack Helyer (6)	144
Keeley Butters (6)	145

Peel Park Primary School, Bradford

Emily Booth (6)	146
Zara Khan (6)	147
Hafsa Malik (7)	148
Hibah Naeem (7)	149
Mahbub Ali (7)	150

St Joseph's Catholic Primary School, Rossington

Luke Rogowski (6)	151
Michael Scarborough (6)	152
Bonnie Taylor (6)	153
Ellie Mae Rainsbury (6)	154
Jonathan Docherty (6)	155
Isabelle Brookes (6)	156
Abigail Charlotte Ross (6)	157
Zack Skinn (7)	158
Ruby Midgley (7)	159
Dylan Jack Bee (6)	160
Kobi Bond (6)	161
Daneesh Madapatha (7)	162
Archie Clark (6)	163
James Michael Summers (6)	164

St Luke's CE Primary School, Bradford

Hughie Groark (6)	165
Szymon Marcinkowski	166
Oscar Marks (6)	167

THE POEMS

What Am I?

I look like a head.
I look like stew with bogeys in.
I taste like dead fleas and shark slime.
I taste like slimy slugs and worms.
I look like slime.
I smell like a rotten turnip.
How slimy I am!
What am I?

Answer: Slime stew.

Layton Mark Abblett (6)
Anlaby Primary School, Hull

Riddle Me This

I taste like slippery eels.
How roary I am!
I look soft and fluffy.
I will bite.
I scratch.
I am creepy.
I have black spots on me.
I have spikes in me.
What am I?

Answer: An animal stew.

Tyler Burrluck (7)
Anlaby Primary School, Hull

Riddle Me This

I am slimy and muddy.
How pink I am!
I like to wriggle about.
Some people like me.
Some people don't like me.
I am friends with bugs.
I am very, very long.
What am I?

Answer: A superworm.

Isabella Rimmer (6)
Anlaby Primary School, Hull

A Rotten Riddle

I have little bugs inside of me.
I have sloppy blood in me.
I have flies flying around me.
I am cold, not warm.
What a revolting recipe I am!
Do you want to eat me?
What am I?

Answer: Rotten soup.

Nicolé Howley (6)
Anlaby Primary School, Hull

Riddle Me This

I have worms inside of me.
I am wrapped in foil.
I look disgusting and revolting.
What a disgusting food I am!
I have mud inside of me.
I feel slimy and muddy.
What am I?

Answer: A mud pie.

Jessica Imogen Overfield (6)
Anlaby Primary School, Hull

My Disgusting Riddle

I am full of gritty candyfloss.
How dirty I am!
I have got juicy worms in me.
I am dirty and black inside.
I am the same on the outside.
How yucky I am!
What am I?

Answer: A dirt delight.

Ruby Brooks (7)
Anlaby Primary School, Hull

My Disgusting Riddle

I am filled with mud and bugs.
I smell like a pig.
Do you want to eat me?
How rotten I am!
I have lots of mud in me.
I have hundreds of bugs in me.
What am I?

Answer: A mud pie.

Matthew White (6)
Anlaby Primary School, Hull

Riddle Me

I am snotty and full of creepy-crawlies.
How revolting I am!
I am wonderful to eat.
How smelly I am!
I am cold and rotten.
I have slugs in me.
What am I?

Answer: A mud pie.

Lily Blair (6)
Anlaby Primary School, Hull

What Am I?

I feel sloppy and squishy.
I look brown and slimy.
I smell mouldy and stinky.
I taste disgusting and gross.
I have rotten, green lumps.
What am I?

Answer: A rotten fish stew.

Ryan Fletcher (6)
Anlaby Primary School, Hull

What Am I?

I have red all over me.
I have green leaves on my head.
I am cold when you eat me.
I am a berry.
How cold I am!
How red I am!
What am I?

Answer: A strawberry.

Savannah Goodfellow (6)
Anlaby Primary School, Hull

What Am I?

I am smooth on the outside.
I am tasty and crunchy on the inside.
You can bake me.
I am drippy.
I am tasty.
I have mud in me.
What am I?

Answer: A mud pie.

Maya Casey (6)
Anlaby Primary School, Hull

A Revolting Riddle

I am full of nuts.
I am yummy.
I am so slimy.
How rotten I am!
How revolting I am!
Would you like to eat me?
What am I?

Answer: A slug poo pie.

Amelia Stubbs (6)
Anlaby Primary School, Hull

Riddle Me

I am red with some green in me.
How revolting I am!
I am purple and a little orange.
How smelly I am!
Do you want to eat me?
What am I?

Answer: Worm soup.

Theo Lee (6)
Anlaby Primary School, Hull

What Am I?

I smell like rotten cheese.
I have slime on me.
I have Goofy socks on.
I look slimy and bubbly.
How wet I am!
What am I?

Answer: Slimy Goofy socks.

Libby Winter (6)
Anlaby Primary School, Hull

Riddle Me

I am so revolting.
I have black, muddy toenails.
I have sticks and crunchy bugs.
I have squidgy mud.
How smelly I am!
What am I?

Answer: A toenail pie.

Oliver Fitzsimmons (6)
Anlaby Primary School, Hull

Rotten Riddle!

I am so revolting.
I am so rotten.
I have stinky eggs.
I am so sloppy.
I am so disgusting.
How smelly I am!
What am I?

Answer: A rotten pancake.

Doll Peaches (6)
Anlaby Primary School, Hull

What Am I?

I taste crunchy and hot.
I look slippery and muddy.
How smooth I am!
I am round.
I have worms in me.
I am hard.
What am I?

Answer: A mud pie.

Faith Ellerington (7)
Anlaby Primary School, Hull

Riddle Me

I am cold not warm.
How cold I am!
I am full of bugs.
You won't want me for dinner.
I am rotten and frozen.
What am I?

Answer: Slug ice cream.

Romi Western (6)
Anlaby Primary School, Hull

Rotten Riddle

I am so revolting.
I look like a nice pie.
I have toenails inside of me.
How smelly I am!
I am cold, not warm.
What am I?

Answer: A toenail pie.

Quinn Graham (6)
Anlaby Primary School, Hull

Revolting

I am full of worms and woodlice.
I have creatures in me.
I am full of mud.
I have slime inside of me.
What am I?

Answer: A mud pie.

Alexander Logan Sanders (6)
Anlaby Primary School, Hull

Revolting Recipe Riddle

How sticky I am!
What a revolting recipe I am!
How slimy I am!
How smelly I am!
How cold I am!
What am I?

Answer: A mud pie.

Jared Morgan (6)
Anlaby Primary School, Hull

Rotten Riddle

I am muddy and sloppy.
I am full of rotten slugs.
I am big when you look at me.
How smelly I am!
What am I?

Answer: A mud pie.

Aarrison Morris (7)
Anlaby Primary School, Hull

We Sting You

I taste stingy and horrible.
Put me in your mouth and I will sting you like mad.
I feel revolting.
What am I?

Answer: A wasp stew.

Chloe Edge (7)
Anlaby Primary School, Hull

What Am I?

I am spongy.
I taste horrible.
I feel lumpy.
I am gross.
I pop when you bite me.
What am I?

Answer: An eyeball pudding.

Ollie Soper (6)
Anlaby Primary School, Hull

Revolting Riddle

I am full of stinky things.
I am full of hard bugs.
I am full of worms.
I am full of seeds.
What am I?

Answer: A mud pie.

Callum James Mainprize (6)
Anlaby Primary School, Hull

What Am I?

I am chewy.
Everyone likes me.
I smell yummy.
I taste delicious.
I will make you poorly.
What am I?

Answer: Sweets.

Lottie Appleyard (6)
Anlaby Primary School, Hull

Rotten Riddle

I have horrible muddy worms.
I am sloppy.
I am wormy.
I am sticky.
How squishy I am.
What am I?

Answer: Mud pie.

Saffron Annabelle Jones (6)
Anlaby Primary School, Hull

Revolting Recipe Riddle

I am sloppy and slimy.
I am red with worms in.
I am revolting.
How squishy I am!
What am I?

Answer: A slug pie.

Holly Danby (6)
Anlaby Primary School, Hull

What Am I?

I taste slimy and sloppy.
I am not a normal soup.
I am revolting.
I am stinky.
What am I?

Answer: Eyeball soup.

Reuben Houlder (6)
Anlaby Primary School, Hull

What Am I?

I taste very funny.
I feel like a mud pie.
I look disgusting.
I smell stinky.
What am I?

Answer: A cheese stew.

Edward Hill (6)
Anlaby Primary School, Hull

What Am I?

I am good for you.
How wonderful I am!
I am the best.
I make you better.
What am I?

Answer: A plum.

Evie Minns (6)
Anlaby Primary School, Hull

What Am I?

I taste bubbly and lovely.
I look like a volcano.
I feel soft and brown.
What am I?

Answer: A soap cake.

Scarlett Fitzsimmons (6)
Anlaby Primary School, Hull

Rotten Riddle

I have rotten eggs.
I am brown and wet.
I am stinky and slimy.
What am I?

Answer: A mud pie.

Abbie Sullivan-Coles (6)
Anlaby Primary School, Hull

Disgusting Riddle

I am disgusting.
I am stinky.
I am big.
I am slimy.
What am I?

Answer: A mud pie.

Oscar Swailes (6)
Anlaby Primary School, Hull

What Am I?

Sometimes I eat smelly cheese because it is tasty.
I live in a house and underground so I can hide from people.
My tail is as soft as a piece of string
And my body is as soft as a bear.
I am easy to catch because you can set up a trap.
I am in the cartoon called 'Tom and Jerry'.
What am I?

Answer: A mouse.

Mia Elizabeth Armstrong (6)
Bedale CE Primary School, Bedale

What Am I?

I am a herbivore.
I like to eat leaves and vegetables.
I live in Africa where it is hot.
I like to run around to see new places.
I am as soft as a teddy.
A carnivore can eat me.
An omnivore can eat me.
I cannot eat them.
I have black and white stripes.
What am I?

Answer: A zebra.

Amy Louise Draper (6)
Bedale CE Primary School, Bedale

What Am I?

I have tiny feet and a thin body.
I live in woodland and trees.
Sometimes I live in houses.
I am a herbivore, I eat fruit and seeds.
I also like to eat cheese.
I don't like being chased by cats.
You can't see me because I am tiny.
What am I?

Answer: A mouse.

Amy Hannington (6)
Bedale CE Primary School, Bedale

What Am I?

I am as black as the sky at night.
I have very sharp teeth that are like knives.
I am as furry as a rabbit
But I have a longer tail.
I live with a person
But I hunt for mice.
I like to eat my treats as they are yummy.
What am I?

Answer: A cat.

Emmy Stinson (6)
Bedale CE Primary School, Bedale

What Am I?

I am a herbivore
And I like to eat leaves.
I live in Africa
And I like to roll in the grass.
I am fluffy and soft
Just like a teddy.
Carnivores can eat me
But I cannot eat them.
I have black and white stripes.
What am I?

Answer: A zebra.

Beatrice Hayes (6)
Bedale CE Primary School, Bedale

What Am I?

I have black spots like a cheetah.
I can run very fast and I am furry.
I live in Africa in the wild.
I eat lots of grass and meat.
I am a carnivore.
I like to drink a lot of water.
I have little legs and a long tail.
What am I?

Answer: A hyena.

William Hearne (6)
Bedale CE Primary School, Bedale

What Am I?

I am like blue water.
Sometimes I come after you.
I live in the Pacific Ocean.
I am a carnivore.
I eat meat and fish.
I like swimming every day.
I hunt for my prey.
I am a character in 'Finding Nemo'.
What am I?

Answer: A shark.

Alfie Coxon (6)
Bedale CE Primary School, Bedale

What Am I?

I am the biggest cat in the world.
I can run very fast.
I am a meat eater.
I am a good swimmer.
You can't keep me as a pet.
I have different stripes to my friends.
I have sharp teeth.
I have sharp claws.
What am I?

Answer: A tiger.

Freddie Cuthbert (5)
Bedale CE Primary School, Bedale

What Am I?

I have black and yellow dots.
I am a carnivore, I eat meat.
I am one of the fastest creatures.
I can run very fast.
My paws are brown.
I do not mind the heat.
I sleep on the ground.
I have many babies.
What am I?

Answer: A cheetah.

Joshua Gaskell (7)
Bedale CE Primary School, Bedale

What Am I?

I am as soft as a sloth.
I roam across the land for food.
I am spotty like some dogs.
I have very sharp teeth.
I can have blue or brown eyes.
I live in Africa where I run around.
I run as quick as the wind.
What am I?

Answer: A cheetah.

Leah Knight (6)
Bedale CE Primary School, Bedale

Animal Riddle

I can fly in the sky as high as the clouds.
I have bright, colourful colours.
I have a curved beak.
I have bright red eyes.
I have two clawed feet.
You see me in the sky.
Sometimes people teach me to talk.
What am I?

Answer: A parrot.

Walter Oldham (6)
Bedale CE Primary School, Bedale

Animal Riddle

I eat meat and bones as hard as metal.
My home is called a kennel.
My fur is as soft as a feather.
I am hyper like a toddler on a bike.
People are my favourite owners.
Being a stray is very bad!
What am I?

Answer: A dog.

Henry James King (7)
Bedale CE Primary School, Bedale

What Am I?

I am a good swimmer.
My stripes help me camouflage.
You can hear me for miles.
I hunt to find food.
I have fat legs.
I am the largest cat.
I am endangered.
Please don't hurt me.
What am I?

Answer: A tiger.

Kairi Buckton (5)
Bedale CE Primary School, Bedale

What Am I?

I can run very fast.
I eat meat, buffalo, deer and pig.
I can swim very well.
I find food at night.
People hunt for me.
There isn't many of me left.
I am the largest cat on Earth.
What am I?

Answer: A tiger.

Sophia Ava Read (5)
Bedale CE Primary School, Bedale

What Am I?

I am spotty.
I am as tall as a tree.
I have a long neck to reach leaves.
I make a purring noise like a cat.
I am the tallest animal on Earth.
I always walk around.
I live in Africa.
What am I?

Answer: A giraffe.

Evie Tate (6)
Bedale CE Primary School, Bedale

What Am I?

I like to jump and be cheeky.
I swing up in the branches.
I live in the jungle.
My fur is brown.
I can be black or grey.
I live in a family.
I like my friends.
I love bananas.
What am I?

Answer: A monkey.

Sarah Nolan (6)
Bedale CE Primary School, Bedale

What Am I?

I am a very good swimmer.
I eat buffalo and antelope.
I can run very fast.
There isn't many of me left.
I am the largest cat in the world.
I have black and orange stripes.
What am I?

Answer: A tiger.

Ava Furlong (5)
Bedale CE Primary School, Bedale

What Am I?

I have black stripes.
You can hear me anywhere in the jungle.
I am really scary and I might eat you.
I am endangered, you have to look after me.
I am the biggest cat in the world.
What am I?

Answer: A tiger.

Emily Kingdon (5)
Bedale CE Primary School, Bedale

What Am I?

I can growl very loud.
People hunt for me.
I eat buffalo and deer.
I am nearly extinct.
I can swim very well.
I can run very fast.
I am the biggest cat in the world.
What am I?

Answer: A tiger.

Ellie Croft (5)
Bedale CE Primary School, Bedale

What Am I?

I have razor-sharp teeth.
I eat small and big fish.
I live in the Pacific Ocean.
My colour helps me camouflage.
I move through the ocean.
I have a long, sharp nose.
What am I?

Answer: A swordfish.

Freddie Crowe (6)
Bedale CE Primary School, Bedale

What Am I?

I have black stripes.
I can run very fast.
I am a good swimmer.
I have good camouflage.
I am one of the biggest cats on land.
You can hear my roar from 30 metres away.
What am I?

Answer: A tiger.

Jakob Neate (5)
Bedale CE Primary School, Bedale

Animal Riddle

I am a really good friend.
I have a very long tail.
I like going for walks.
I live in a house.
I like to play fetch.
I have four legs.
I am hyper like a baby.
What am I?

Answer: A dog.

Ava Mollie Prisk (6)
Bedale CE Primary School, Bedale

What Am I?

I am furry like a blanket.
I live in woodland.
I am a carnivore.
I eat meat.
I like to hunt my prey.
I can climb trees.
I like to hunt.
I am in a pack.
What am I?

Answer: A wolf.

Theo Kenny (6)
Bedale CE Primary School, Bedale

What Am I?

My colour helps me camouflage.
My name gives away what I look like.
I like to eat yummy fish.
I live in the sea.
I like to hunt for food.
My nose is sharp.
What am I?

Answer: A swordfish.

Sydney Schofield (6)
Bedale CE Primary School, Bedale

What Am I?

I can run very fast.
You will see me at night.
I can swim very well.
I eat pigs, buffalo and deer.
People hunt for me.
There isn't many of me left.
What am I?

Answer: A tiger.

Zach Main (5)
Bedale CE Primary School, Bedale

What Am I?

I can run very fast in the night.
I am the biggest wildcat.
I am a good swimmer.
I am a meat eater.
I am orange and black.
I have sharp teeth and claws.
What am I?

Answer: A tiger.

Wilf Monkhouse (5)
Bedale CE Primary School, Bedale

What Am I?

I am grey and pink.
Cats chase me a lot.
People fiddle with my tail.
I live in barns and houses.
I like eating chocolate and cheese.
I scare people.
What am I?

Answer: A mouse.

Joel Matthew Holloway (6)
Bedale CE Primary School, Bedale

Animal Riddle

I love to eat yummy carrots.
Sometimes I am grey.
Sometimes I am brown.
I live in a cosy hole.
I jump up and down like a spring.
I am very fluffy.
What am I?

Answer: A rabbit.

Esmae Grace Potter (6)
Bedale CE Primary School, Bedale

Animal Riddle

I live in a house.
My bed is a basket.
I have furry skin.
I can run as fast as a bullet.
I can bark as loud as an alarm.
Chewing bones is really fun.
What am I?

Answer: A dog.

Ellis Laing (6)
Bedale CE Primary School, Bedale

What Am I?

My family's stripes are different.
I can run fast.
I eat buffalo, deer and pig.
I can swim very well.
I hunt at night.
I can roar very loud.
What am I?

Answer: A tiger.

Charley Caygill (5)
Bedale CE Primary School, Bedale

Animal Riddle

I live in ponds and on land.
I have four legs and I ribbit.
I eat flies.
I can jump really high.
I have really long legs.
I look slimy and green.
What am I?

Answer: A frog.

Harry William Corner (6)
Bedale CE Primary School, Bedale

What Am I?

I am as fast as lightning.
I can run for miles before I am sleepy.
I am good at catching food.
I live on the African plains.
I am black and yellow.
What am I?

Answer: A cheetah.

Tegan Rachel Selby (6)
Bedale CE Primary School, Bedale

What Am I?

I hunt for food at night.
I can swim very well.
I am the biggest wildcat.
I can run very fast.
I hunt for pigs and deer.
I am stripy and black.
What am I?

Answer: A tiger.

Jesse-James Freddie Watson (5)
Bedale CE Primary School, Bedale

What Am I?

I am a very good swimmer.
I am a very fast runner.
I am a big cat.
I eat meat.
I have different stripes.
I am fierce.
I have sharp teeth.
What am I?

Answer: A tiger.

Isobel Hainge (5)
Bedale CE Primary School, Bedale

What Am I?

I have a long tail.
I live in the dark ocean.
I am a carnivore.
I eat meat, seals and people.
I have 300 razor-sharp teeth.
I am very scary.
What am I?

Answer: A shark.

James Dickinson (6)
Bedale CE Primary School, Bedale

What Am I?

I swim very well.
I can run very fast.
I eat buffalo and deer.
I roar very loud.
I have black and yellow stripes.
I hunt for food at night.
What am I?

Answer: A tiger.

Fraya Pritchard (6)
Bedale CE Primary School, Bedale

What Am I?

I have stripes.
I am a good swimmer.
My stripes make me camouflage.
I am endangered.
My stripes are different.
I am the biggest cat.
What am I?

Answer: A tiger.

Poppy Grace King (5)
Bedale CE Primary School, Bedale

Animal Riddle

I fly like a parrot.
I can sleep upside down.
I can see in the dark.
My teeth point down.
I live in a cave.
I eat flies and insects.
What am I?

Answer: A bat.

Ava Waldron (6)
Bedale CE Primary School, Bedale

What Am I?

I hunt at night.
I am very good at swimming.
I can run fast.
I have different stripes.
I have sharp teeth.
I am orange and black.
What am I?

Answer: A tiger.

Harri James (5)
Bedale CE Primary School, Bedale

What Am I?

I eat buffalo, deer and pig.
I can swim very well.
I can run fast.
I can roar loudly.
I am orange and black.
People hunt for me.
What am I?

Answer: A tiger.

Jessica Louise Scarce (5)
Bedale CE Primary School, Bedale

What Am I?

I am green with dark spots.
I can be as small as a hedgehog.
I am slimy and I jump about.
I have lots of bubbles.
I live in a river.
What am I?

Answer: A frog.

Courtney Cooper (6)
Bedale CE Primary School, Bedale

What Am I?

I eat crickets.
I can stick to stuff.
I can be camouflaged.
I live on mountains.
I like to lie on hot rocks.
I run fast.
What am I?

Answer: A lizard.

Arthur Nicholson (6)
Bedale CE Primary School, Bedale

What Am I?

I can swim very well.
I hunt at night for food.
I can run very fast.
I eat buffalo, pigs and deer.
I like to drink water.
What am I?

Answer: A tiger.

Harry Balsillie (5)
Bedale CE Primary School, Bedale

What Am I?

I am the king of the cat family.
I have different stripes to my family.
I am good at swimming.
I roar very loudly.
I eat meat.
What am I?

Answer: A tiger.

Payson Carney (5)
Bedale CE Primary School, Bedale

What Am I?

I can run fast.
I am a good swimmer.
I am a big cat.
I eat pigs and deer.
My stripes are different.
I am a meat eater.
What am I?

Answer: A tiger.

Katie-Beth Miller (5)
Bedale CE Primary School, Bedale

Animal Riddle

I am as black as the night sky.
I sleep in a dark, gloomy cave.
My teeth are as sharp as razors.
I fly like a little bird.
What am I?

Answer: A bat.

Freya Doyle (6)
Bedale CE Primary School, Bedale

What Am I?

I can swim very fast.
I can run very fast.
I hunt at night.
I like to eat buffalo.
I like deer.
I am stripy.
What am I?

Answer: A tiger.

Mason Tuplin (5)
Bedale CE Primary School, Bedale

Animal Riddle

I have long legs.
I have a fluffy body.
I can crawl up the wall.
I can crawl under things.
I have a sparkly web.
What am I?

Answer: A spider.

Abby Stewart (6)
Bedale CE Primary School, Bedale

What Am I?

I have a big trunk.
I am bigger than a lion.
I live in a forest.
I drink lots of water.
I eat leaves.
What am I?

Answer: An elephant.

Jack Allen (6)
Bedale CE Primary School, Bedale

What Am I?

I hunt at night.
I can swim very well.
I can run very fast.
I eat buffalo and pigs.
I have stripy skin.
What am I?

Answer: A tiger.

Tiana Mae Merkin (5)
Bedale CE Primary School, Bedale

What Am I?

I am a good swimmer.
I like to eat meat.
I like to run fast.
I am the biggest cat.
I have stripy fur.
What am I?

Answer: A tiger.

Sam Simpson (5)
Bedale CE Primary School, Bedale

What Am I?

I like to eat meat.
I can be camouflaged.
I am a big cat.
I am a good swimmer.
I have stripes.
What am I?

Answer: A tiger.

Grace Lily Kent (5)
Bedale CE Primary School, Bedale

Animal Riddle

I have fourteen legs.
I get under rocks.
I like to eat leaves and plants.
My eggs hatch on my tummy.
What am I?

Answer: A woodlouse.

Levi Chilcott (6)
Bedale CE Primary School, Bedale

What Am I?

I have stripes.
I can catch my prey.
I roll around in the grass.
I eat meat.
I am the biggest cat.
What am I?

Answer: A tiger.

Heather Elsie Hobson (6)
Bedale CE Primary School, Bedale

Animal Riddle

I live in Africa.
Sometimes lions eat me.
I stand up on rocks.
I have brown skin.
I am fluffy.
What am I?

Answer: A meerkat.

Abigail Dakota Butterworth (6)
Bedale CE Primary School, Bedale

What Am I?

I am a good swimmer.
I eat meat for my tea.
I can roar very loud.
My friends have different stripes.
What am I?

Answer: A tiger.

Sophia Teer (5)
Bedale CE Primary School, Bedale

What Am I?

I run very fast.
I like to eat meat.
I like to swim.
I have a loud roar.
I am the biggest cat.
What am I?

Answer: A tiger.

Sienna Kirkley (5)
Bedale CE Primary School, Bedale

What Am I?

I have stripes.
My stripes make me camouflage.
I can roar loudly.
I am a big cat.
I like meat.
What am I?

Answer: A tiger.

Kira Graham (5)
Bedale CE Primary School, Bedale

Animal Riddle

I live in the ocean.
I sometimes eat bacon.
I sometimes pinch you.
I can be found on the beach.
What am I?

Answer: A crab.

Evie Graham (6)
Bedale CE Primary School, Bedale

Animal Riddle

I live with other animals in the jungle.
I can live in the desert sometimes.
I can run very fast.
What am I?

Answer: A cheetah.

Thomas Cope (6)
Bedale CE Primary School, Bedale

What Am I?

I am stripy.
I am black and white.
I like to run fast.
During the day I like to play.
What am I?

Answer: A zebra.

Olivia Harker (6)
Bedale CE Primary School, Bedale

What Am I?

I am stripy.
I can run fast.
I have a fierce roar.
I love meat.
I am a big cat.
What am I?

Answer: A tiger.

Emily Rebecca Taylor (5)
Bedale CE Primary School, Bedale

What Am I?

I have stripes.
I eat meat.
I hunt at night.
I swim fast.
I run fast.
What am I?

Answer: A tiger.

Oscar Byers (5)
Bedale CE Primary School, Bedale

What Am I?

I can swim.
I can run fast.
I can eat deer.
What am I?

Answer: A tiger.

Jack Thornton-Grace (5)
Bedale CE Primary School, Bedale

What Am I?

I can swim.
I roar loudly.
I eat meat.
What am I?

Answer: A tiger.

Mia-Louise Fitch (5)
Bedale CE Primary School, Bedale

Fluttering Flyers

These creatures are fluttering flyers.
These creatures are secret stealers.
These creatures are night sneakers.
These creatures are teeth builders.
These creatures are coin returners.
These creatures are twinkling spies.
Who are they?

Answer: The tooth fairies.

Ally Johnson (7)
Golden Flatts Primary School, Hartlepool

Fork Tongue

I am sometimes short.
People are often scared of me.
My tongue is like a fork.
I have scales that never weigh.
I can shed my skin.
I can be big.
I like to climb.
I have no legs.
What am I?

Answer: A snake.

Taio Hill-Bate (6)
Golden Flatts Primary School, Hartlepool

Pick Of The Bunch

I am a funny shape.
People like me.
I can be peeled.
I am full of carbohydrates.
You can eat me.
My coat is yellow.
I taste delicious.
I am a healthy snack.
What am I?

Answer: A banana.

Darcie Davies (7)
Golden Flatts Primary School, Hartlepool

Flow Free

I have a bed but never sleep.
I can run for miles.
My mouth is small.
I am the habitat for many.
You can swim in me in summer.
I often freeze in the winter.
What am I?

Answer: A river.

Lydia Evans (6)
Golden Flatts Primary School, Hartlepool

Blower

(A kennings poem)

Tree blower.
Cloud taker.
Bush mover.
Leaf breaker.
Windmill spinner.
People shaker.
Cold bringer.
Electricity maker.
What am I?

Answer: *The wind.*

Abbie Morris (7)
Golden Flatts Primary School, Hartlepool

The Little Tinker

(A kennings poem)

Silent creeper.
Coin giver.
Window sneaker.
Night flyer.
Secret stranger.
Sparkling winger.
Who am I?

Answer: The tooth fairy.

Amelia-Mai Pearson (7)
Golden Flatts Primary School, Hartlepool

A Rocky Mountain

(A kennings poem)

Lava rocketer.
Magma burster.
Fire thrower.
Rock slider.
City melter.
Scorching erupter.
What am I?

Answer: A volcano.

Lucianna Ness (7)
Golden Flatts Primary School, Hartlepool

A Yellow Flash

(A kennings poem)

Flash lighter.
Quick clicker.
Sheep scarer.
Huge flyer.
Giant crasher.
Tree zapper.
What am I?

Answer: Lightning.

Grace Olivia Bell (7)
Golden Flatts Primary School, Hartlepool

Best Friend

(A kennings poem)

Fur cleaner.
Cat scarer.
Stick chaser.
Postman racer.
Bone licker.
Letter ripper.
What am I?

Answer: A dog.

Louis Michael Souter (7)
Golden Flatts Primary School, Hartlepool

Chomping Chew

I have pointy teeth.
I have a fin.
I live underwater.
I blow bubbles like a fish.
I am blue and orange.
I am medium-sized.
I have no feet.
I don't like flowers.
My name starts with 'P'.
What am I?

Answer: A piranha.

Jamie Atkinson (5)
King Street Primary School, Spennymoor

What Am I?

I come in the winter.
I am as still as a statue.
I crumple when I get made.
I have a carrot as a nose.
I shiver in the cold.
What am I?

Answer: A snowman.

Jenson Horniman (6)
King Street Primary School, Spennymoor

What Am I?

I live in the trees in the rainforest.
I jump from tree to tree.
I am orange.
I have fur.
I have two feet.
I have two hands.
What am I?

Answer: An orangutan.

Elliott Bright (5)
King Street Primary School, Spennymoor

The Leaf Muncher

I eat leaves.
I have a long tongue.
I have patches.
I have horns.
I have eyes.
I have long eyelashes.
I have a long neck.
What am I?

Answer: A giraffe.

Nell Beasley (6)
King Street Primary School, Spennymoor

The Tiny Scratcher

I drink milk.
I am a pet.
I climb trees.
I am as fluffy as a teddy.
I sleep in the sun all day.
I am as cute as a puppy.
What am I?

Answer: A kitten.

Tabitha Violet Daley (5)
King Street Primary School, Spennymoor

Legs

I crawl on the floor like a mouse.
I am small but I can sting you.
I am black all over my body.
I am silent like a ninja.
What am I?

Answer: An ant.

Harry Luther (5)
King Street Primary School, Spennymoor

Who Am I?

I might have a gun.
I help people.
I wear a uniform.
I drive a car.
I wear a hat.
I catch baddies.
Who am I?

Answer: A policeman.

Jake David Murdoch (5)
King Street Primary School, Spennymoor

What Am I?

I am cute.
I like fetching balls.
I like to take naps.
I bury my balls.
I am good at sniffing things out.
What am I?

Answer: A puppy.

Willow Flatman (5)
King Street Primary School, Spennymoor

What Am I?

I have black stripes.
I am orange.
I have claws on my feet.
I eat meat.
I am angry.
I can run fast.
What am I?

Answer: A tiger.

Blake Robert Barnes (6)
King Street Primary School, Spennymoor

What Am I?

I am grey.
I like to hang on trees.
I move slowly.
I am as soft as a bear.
I live in the rainforest.
What am I?

Answer: A sloth.

Katharine Gardner (5)
King Street Primary School, Spennymoor

Guess What I Am?

I bark all night.
I have four legs.
I have fur.
I like to eat dog food.
I like to play with footballs.
What am I?

Answer: A dog.

Alfie-Shay Simpson (5)
King Street Primary School, Spennymoor

The Tiny Barker

I am as tiny as a bird.
I am as soft as a blanket.
I bark when I see someone.
I lick people.
What am I?

Answer: A puppy.

Kellan Bates (5)
King Street Primary School, Spennymoor

Guess What?

We are wet and slimy.
We live in the soil.
We are good for the soil.
We are pink.
What are we?

Answer: Worms.

Amelie Elliott (5)
King Street Primary School, Spennymoor

Guess What I Am?

I am cold.
I am put into water.
I melt in hot water.
You can see me in winter.
What am I?

Answer: Ice.

Amelia Dixon (5)
King Street Primary School, Spennymoor

What Am I?

I miaow in the morning.
I have four legs.
I chase mice.
I like lots of naps.
What am I?

Answer: A cat.

Cayden Dodds (5)
King Street Primary School, Spennymoor

Guess What I Am?

I am as black as a tyre.
I eat bread.
I can fly around.
I live in a nest.
What am I?

Answer: A bird.

Scarlett Ellis (5)
King Street Primary School, Spennymoor

What Am I?

I bark all night.
I like going for a walk.
I walk in a park.
I have fur.
What am I?

Answer: A dog.

Danny Summerson (5)
King Street Primary School, Spennymoor

What Am I?

I wake up in the night.
I sleep in a tree.
I have feathers.
I can fly.
What am I?

Answer: An owl.

Sophia Cathrine Janette Byrne (5)
King Street Primary School, Spennymoor

What Am I?

I eat lots of food.
I walk slowly.
I am black like soil.
I am tiny.
What am I?

Answer: An ant.

Phoebe Cullum (5)
King Street Primary School, Spennymoor

What Am I?

I have green skin.
I can jump.
I eat fish.
I have four legs.
What am I?

Answer: A frog.

Hayden Parker (5)
King Street Primary School, Spennymoor

Secret

I can send water around me.
I can attack my prey.
I can live for up to eighty years.
Sometimes you can't see me.
I live in warm places like Africa.
I can eat leaves.
I have four legs.
What am I?

Answer: A turtle.

Ethan Jack Harrison (6)
Our Lady Of The Most Holy Rosary RC Primary School, Billingham

I Am An Animal

I have two ears and one tail.
I have four paws and four legs.
I have white skin and brown fur.
My paws are white and black.
You can take me for a walk.
You can wash me in a little bath.
What am I?

Answer: A chihuahua.

Jessica Caitlyn Bruce (6)
Our Lady Of The Most Holy Rosary RC Primary School, Billingham

What Am I?

I am red and blue.
I have legs.
I have a sensor.
Some people are terrified of me.
I can spin webs and stick to walls.
I share my power with people.
I am a minibeast.
What am I?

Answer: A spider.

Zak Georgiou (6)
Our Lady Of The Most Holy Rosary RC Primary School, Billingham

The Animal Riddle

I am an animal.
I am as big and grey as an elephant.
I am hunted for something.
I am not seen in Britain.
I have a horn on me.
What am I?

Answer: A rhino.

Caitlin Louise Black (7)
Our Lady Of The Most Holy Rosary RC Primary School, Billingham

What Am I?

I am a minibeast.
I am all sorts of colours.
I live in different countries.
I am normally in forests.
I can fly.
What am I?

Answer: A butterfly.

Georgia Catherine Jackson (6)
Our Lady Of The Most Holy Rosary RC Primary School, Billingham

What Am I?

I am black.
I like trees.
I make a nest.
I sit in my nest each day.
I have a black beak.
I like shiny stuff.
What am I?

Answer: A magpie.

William Sotheby (6)
Our Lady Of The Most Holy Rosary RC Primary School, Billingham

What Am I?

I am brown.
I have four legs.
I have whiskers.
I walk home.
I have teeth.
I have ears.
I have brown eyes.
What am I?

Answer: A dog.

Tyler Leighton-Spence (6)
Our Lady Of The Most Holy Rosary RC Primary School, Billingham

Am I An Animal?

I have four legs.
I can hide from my prey.
I can camouflage in grass.
I can roar loudly.
I live in the forest.
What am I?

Answer: A tiger.

Mateusz Michal Odziomek (7)
Our Lady Of The Most Holy Rosary RC Primary School, Billingham

What Am I?

I am a slimy land animal.
I hang off trees.
I go in grass.
I slither about.
I hiss when people come near me.
What am I?

Answer: A snake.

Oliver Evans (6)
Our Lady Of The Most Holy Rosary RC Primary School, Billingham

What Am I?

I live in a cave.
I go up to the surface.
I have a tail.
I have hair.
I have friends.
What am I?

Answer: A mermaid.

Zara (6)
Our Lady Of The Most Holy Rosary RC Primary School, Billingham

What Am I?

I am slithery and slimy.
I can climb walls.
I am like a snake.
Kids are mostly scared of me.
What am I?

Answer: A slug.

Freddie Harrison (6)
Our Lady Of The Most Holy Rosary RC Primary School, Billingham

What Am I?

I have four legs.
I am stripy.
I have a long tail.
I am very scary.
I am very big.
What am I?

Answer: A tiger.

Jade Cater (6)
Our Lady Of The Most Holy Rosary RC Primary School, Billingham

Soft Animal

I live in the Arctic.
I am not furry.
I hunt for fish.
I am black and white.
What am I?

Answer: A penguin.

Harry Faso (6)
Our Lady Of The Most Holy Rosary RC Primary School, Billingham

What Am I?

The sun is golden like jewels.
The water is blue like the sky.
The sand is golden.
What am I?

Answer: A beach.

Samuel Turnbull (6)
Our Lady Of The Most Holy Rosary RC Primary School, Billingham

What Am I?

I have ears.
I have blue eyes.
I have a pink tail.
I have a horn.
What am I?

Answer: A unicorn.

Bayleigh Jasmine Violet Henderson (6)
Our Lady Of The Most Holy Rosary RC Primary School, Billingham

What Am I?

I have 100 legs.
I am brown.
I am long.
I am a minibeast.
What am I?

Answer: A centipede.

Matthew Jack Helyer (6)
Our Lady Of The Most Holy Rosary RC Primary School, Billingham

What Am I?

I can fly.
I am shiny.
I am pink.
I have a horn.
What am I?

Answer: A unicorn.

Keeley Butters (6)
Our Lady Of The Most Holy Rosary RC Primary School, Billingham

Galloping Fast On A Quest To The End Of The World

I live in a stable that looks like a cave.
I eat golden hay in the middle of the day.
I have a mane that gets wet in the rain.
I run as fast as a cheetah.
I can win a race and a bet.
I don't like loud noises.
I come in different colours.
I get a snack when I am good.
What am I?

Answer: A horse.

Emily Booth (6)
Peel Park Primary School, Bradford

The Cutie Who Likes Cake

He eats and eats and eats because he likes his treats.
His tummy is so big that he can't dig.
He is white and fluffy but ever so lumpy.
He is cute and likes cakes but he just takes and takes!
What is he?

Answer: A greedy rabbit.

Zara Khan (6)
Peel Park Primary School, Bradford

Can Be A Computer Too

I am a ball that you don't play with.
You can cut me into pieces.
I am the alternative to a doctor.
You can taste me.
I start with 'ap'.
What am I?

Answer: An apple.

Hafsa Malik (7)
Peel Park Primary School, Bradford

Little Monster

I can fight and roll into a ball.
I have a pointy tongue
and sharp teeth.
I have black and green eyes.
I live under rocks.
What am I?

Answer: A snake.

Hibah Naeem (7)
Peel Park Primary School, Bradford

Colour Changer!

I come in many colours.
I sway when I walk.
I have four legs.
I have a spiky back.
What am I?

Answer: A chameleon.

Mahbub Ali (7)
Peel Park Primary School, Bradford

Big Trees

It is made up of lots of trees,
they are very tall and green.
There are lots of animals that live here,
some can be fierce, some can be mean.
There are monkeys here too,
they like to swing and play.
There are lots of strange noises you can
hear here all day.
This is a good home for creepy-crawlies
and hissing snakes too.
I don't think I would visit here alone,
would you?
What is it?

Answer: A jungle.

Luke Rogowski (6)
St Joseph's Catholic Primary School, Rossington

A Squeak And A Peek

I squeak and peek
and come out every week.
My ears are pink
and my nose is round.
My legs are small
but my tail is long.
I like to sit on my knees
and eat lots of cheese.
I like to crawl through
and have a nice chew.
I run away from the cat
as fast as a black bat.
What am I?

Answer: A mouse.

Michael Scarborough (6)
St Joseph's Catholic Primary School, Rossington

Cuckoo!

My numbers, they are few.
My hands, well I have two.
My face is sometimes round
but I never wear a frown.
You can take me anywhere.
You can see me from your armchair.
Tick-tock, tick-tock, I go.
Even when I am running slow.
What am I?

Answer: A clock.

Bonnie Taylor (6)
St Joseph's Catholic Primary School, Rossington

Ellie's Little Kingdom

Sometimes I am big.
Sometimes I am small.
Sometimes I am little.
Sometimes I am tall.
You see me every day.
You can't pick me up or take me away.
If the windows are open the wind will blow.
I will keep you warm in the rain or snow.
What am I?

Answer: A house.

Ellie Mae Rainsbury (6)
St Joseph's Catholic Primary School, Rossington

Shader

You can use it hot or cold.
It is not good in the wind.
It might turn inside out.
It goes up but it is not a plane.
It gets wet but it is not a sponge.
It has a handle but it is not a door.
It will help you in the rain and sun.
What is it?

Answer: An umbrella.

Jonathan Docherty (6)
St Joseph's Catholic Primary School, Rossington

For Life, Not Just For Christmas

Just like a baby,
I am as cute as a button.
Covered in fur,
All soft and fluffy.
Naughty and playful.
When I see the postman I go woof.
Sometimes I poo and wee all over the place.
The next minute I am playing chase!
What am I?

Answer: A puppy.

Isabelle Brookes (6)
St Joseph's Catholic Primary School, Rossington

What Am I?

I have a face but no arms.
I am all different shapes and sizes.
Sometimes I am gold or silver.
Sometimes I have a pattern on me.
I have a door or a window.
I am really old.
I am tall.
What am I?

Answer: A grandfather clock.

Abigail Charlotte Ross (6)
St Joseph's Catholic Primary School, Rossington

Look At A Book

I read books but my family don't care.
I wear a red bow in my hair.
I have powers that make the TV bang.
I didn't hear the bell when Miss Honey rang.
My headmistress is as loud as a lion.
Who am I?

Answer: Matilda.

Zack Skinn (7)
St Joseph's Catholic Primary School, Rossington

Juicy Fruit

I am as red as a rose.
You can eat me as a snack.
You can eat me as a dessert.
You can pick me from a field.
I can be sweet or tangy.
I have a green leaf.
I am very juicy.
What am I?

Answer: A strawberry.

Ruby Midgley (7)
St Joseph's Catholic Primary School, Rossington

Yum-Yum In My Tum

I come in different shapes.
I come in different sizes.
I swim in the water.
I can be eaten with potatoes.
I taste delicious with ketchup.
I come wrapped in paper.
What am I?

Answer: Fish and chips.

Dylan Jack Bee (6)
St Joseph's Catholic Primary School, Rossington

What Am I?

My belly fur is five inches thick.
I am native to the rugged highlands.
My tail is almost as long as my body.
60% of us live in China.
I am a beautiful creature.
What am I?

Answer: A snow leopard.

Kobi Bond (6)
St Joseph's Catholic Primary School, Rossington

The Guard Of The Castle!

I can breathe hot, blazing flames.
I have wings to fly high.
I have spiky, black fins.
I am as big as a giant bird.
I always guard castles.
I roar loudly.
What am I?

Answer: A dragon.

Daneesh Madapatha (7)
St Joseph's Catholic Primary School, Rossington

Kickabout

People wearing gloves can pick me up.
I am as round as a wheel.
People play in my team.
I am covered in hexagons.
I am a sphere.
I roll really fast.
What am I?

Answer: A football.

Archie Clark (6)
St Joseph's Catholic Primary School, Rossington

Show Time!

I live on hands.
I make people laugh.
I let people talk for me.
I am a chatterbox.
I like to put on shows.
I have lots of friends.
What am I?

Answer: A puppet.

James Michael Summers (6)
St Joseph's Catholic Primary School, Rossington

What Am I?

I like to use my long tongue
to eat leaves from the top of trees.
I don't have to climb up though,
with my long neck it's a breeze.
I live in Africa, from tall trees I peck,
I am a creature known
for having a long neck.
I have four legs but I am not a chair,
I have a long tongue but I am not a frog.
I eat trees but I am not a koala.
What am I?

Answer: A giraffe.

Hughie Groark (6)
St Luke's CE Primary School, Bradford

Small Shell Ball

Ears are rattling
like a knight in armour battling.
It is as hard as a rock
and its tail goes *clock, clock*.
It curls like a ball
but you can't kick it in a goal.
Sharp claws, small legs, small ears
and a strong tail like spears.
What is it?

Answer: An armadillo.

Szymon Marcinkowski
St Luke's CE Primary School, Bradford

Little Riddlers - The North East

The Mysterious Animal

I am covered in long, brown hair.
My home is in Africa or the zoo.
I am good at climbing trees.
I live in a community or troop.
I sleep high up in a tree.
I talk by grunting.
I don't have a tail.
I am an omnivore.
I have two eyes.
What am I?

Answer: A chimpanzee.

Oscar Marks (6)
St Luke's CE Primary School, Bradford

YoungWriters
Est.1991

YOUNG WRITERS INFORMATION

We hope you have enjoyed reading this book – and that you will continue to in the coming years.

If you're a young writer who enjoys reading and creative writing, or the parent of an enthusiastic poet or story writer, do visit our website **www.youngwriters.co.uk**. Here you will find free competitions, workshops and games, as well as recommended reads, a poetry glossary and our blog.

If you would like to order further copies of this book, or any of our other titles, then please give us a call or visit **www.youngwriters.co.uk**.

Young Writers
Remus House
Coltsfoot Drive
Peterborough
PE2 9BF
(01733) 890066
info@youngwriters.co.uk